Living Fully: Setting Goals with Purpose for 2025 Despite Illness

A guide to embracing life fully and setting meaningful goals, no matter the challenges

Heidi Linegar

Contents

Title: *Living Fully: Setting Goals with Purpose for 2025 Despite Illness*

First Edition

Published by: **Self-Published**

For permission requests, please contact: journeywithheidi@icloud.com

Dedication

To all my friends, family, and my incredible online support network—your love and encouragement have been my strength.

In loving memory of my dear school friend, Kate Duncan, who passed away from cancer at the age of 43. We shared a close bond, and knowing we were on similar journeys breaks my heart, especially as our birthdays were just eight days apart. This book is dedicated to you, Kate, and to all who face this battle with courage.

A heartfelt thanks to the Beacon Centre in Taunton for your care, compassion, and unwavering support during my cancer treatment.

Introduction

Welcome to Living Fully: Setting Goals with Purpose for 2025 Despite Illness.

This book is designed for anyone facing illness or life's unexpected challenges, yet still striving to live each day with purpose and set meaningful goals for the future.

In December 2023, at the age of 43, I was diagnosed with metastatic hormone-positive breast cancer, a life-altering moment. Unlike many, I'm not undergoing chemotherapy or radiotherapy, but instead, I'm receiving CDK 4/6 inhibitors and hormone blockers as part of my treatment. While these medications are keeping the cancer under control, I do experience difficult side effects that often impact my daily life. Additionally, I have been registered blind all my life.

These experiences have shaped my perspective on the importance of living intentionally, setting goals that truly matter, and surrounding myself with a supportive community.

This book is my way of sharing what I've learned. It's for everyone who needs a reminder that life doesn't stop when faced with illness or disability—it becomes an opportunity to embrace each moment, focus on what truly matters, and pursue goals that bring joy and fulfilment.

I know that not everyone loves the word "journey," and I understand why. It's often overused, and it can feel too light a word to describe the difficult and unpredictable paths we walk. But for me, the word "journey" captures the winding, unpredictable nature of life—especially when dealing with illness. It's not a straight line, and it's not always easy, but it's a path we navigate with courage and determination. I hope you'll see it in that way, too: as a reflection of growth, resilience, and change.

Throughout these pages, you'll find strategies for setting achievable goals, reflections on living with illness and disability, and practical steps to make each day count. I hope this book encourages you to live fully, no matter what life throws your way.

Let's begin this journey together, and may 2025 be a year filled with purpose, hope, and new possibilities.

Feel free to make this book your own. In the margins of the lined sections, I've left space for you to add any extra thoughts, reflections, or notes that may come to mind as you work through each chapter. You can also use the margins throughout the book to capture any personal insights or moments of inspiration.

Chapter 1
Overcoming Challenges

Life's Unexpected Hurdles

Life throws many unexpected hurdles our way, especially when you're dealing with illness or other tough obstacles. It's completely natural to feel overwhelmed or uncertain. But I want you to remember that even in the hardest times, there's always an opportunity to grow, discover your inner strength, and keep moving forward—no matter how slow or small those steps might be.

This section is here to help you acknowledge the challenges you're facing and to find ways to overcome them with grace and determination. It's not about rushing through or finding instant solutions, but about recognising your resilience, one moment at a time.

And believe me, I know how it feels when you keep thinking of things to add or reflect on. That's why I've included extra space at the end of the chapter just for you—because if you're anything like me, there's always more to say and process. Feel free to fill those pages with anything that comes to mind, whenever you need.

Big hugs from me as we start this journey together.

1. Acknowledge Your Challenges

Start by naming the specific challenges you're facing. What are the biggest hurdles in your path? Write them down without judgment—acknowledging them is the first step toward overcoming them.

2. Shift Your Perspective

Challenges can often feel overwhelming, but reframing your mindset can make a big difference. Instead of viewing obstacles as roadblocks, try to see them as stepping stones toward growth. Ask yourself:

What can I learn from this situation?

How can I use this challenge to strengthen my resolve?

3. Break It Down

Tackling challenges can feel daunting, but breaking them into smaller, manageable steps can make them feel more achievable. Identify one small action you can take today to address a challenge:

4. Seek Support

You don't have to face challenges alone. Reach out to friends, family, or support groups. Sharing your struggles can lighten the load and often provide new insights. Consider:

Who can I talk to about my challenges?

What resources are available to support me?

5. Practice Self-Compassion

Be gentle with yourself as you navigate challenges. Remember that it's okay to feel frustrated, sad, or overwhelmed at times. Treat yourself with the same kindness you would offer a friend.

- How can I practice self-care during tough times?
- What affirmations can I remind myself of when I'm feeling low?

6. Celebrate Progress

Every step you take, no matter how small, is worth celebrating. Acknowledge your efforts and the progress you make along the way. Consider keeping a journal where you record your victories, big and small:

What is one challenge you faced recently, and how did you overcome it?

What strengths did you discover within yourself during that time?

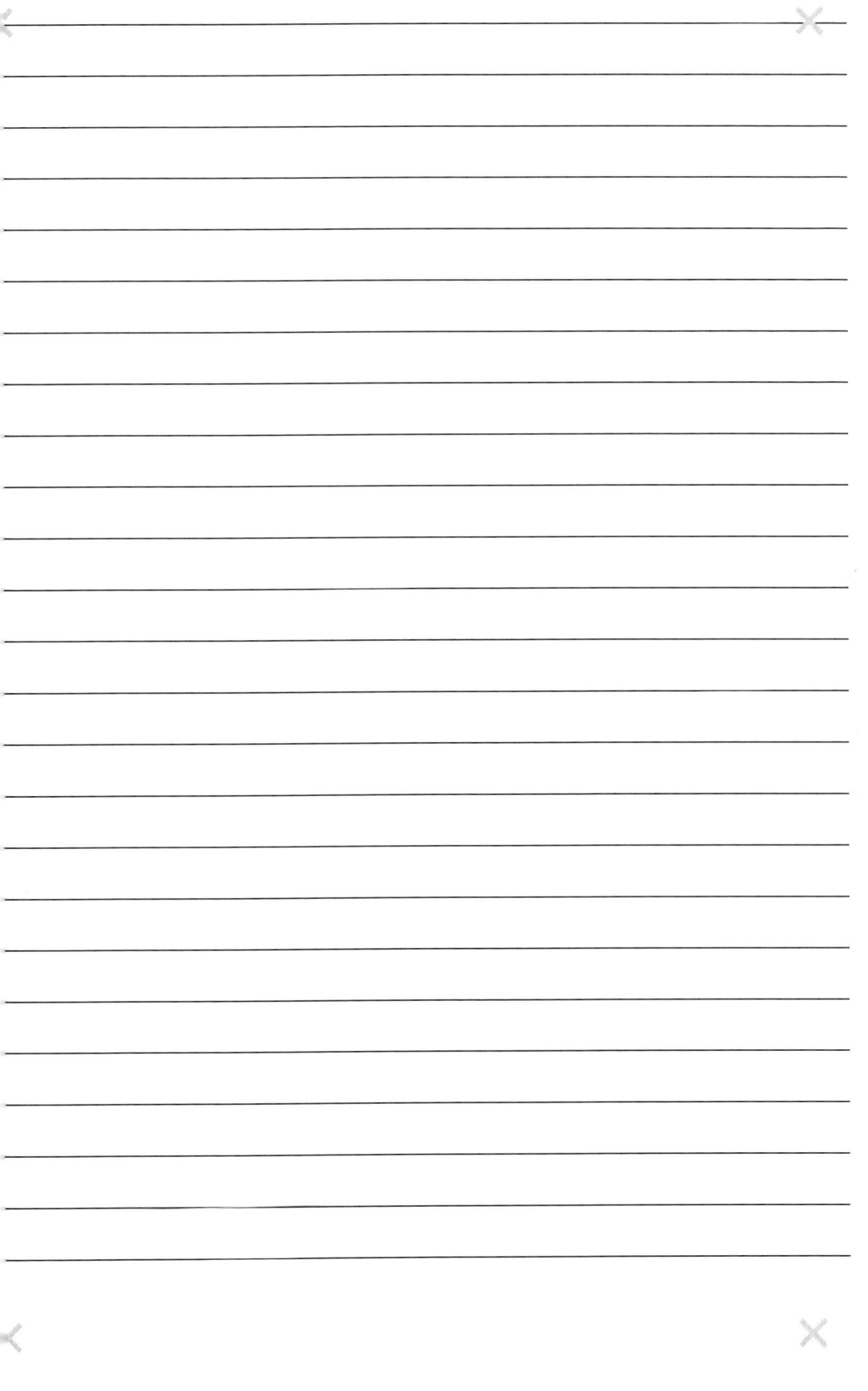

Chapter 2

Navigating Radiotherapy and Chemotherapy

For many individuals undergoing cancer treatment, radiotherapy and chemotherapy are significant parts of the journey. Though I'm not currently receiving these treatments, I know that living with stage 4 cancer means that one day, when my current medications stop working, I may likely face radiotherapy or chemotherapy as my next step. Even though I'm not there yet, I can empathise deeply with those who are on this path. I understand the fears, concerns, and physical and emotional challenges that come with it. Whether you are currently undergoing treatment, preparing for it, or reflecting on your experience, it's important to honour what your body is going through and give yourself the grace and support you need.

Understanding Your Treatment

Radiotherapy and chemotherapy work in different ways to target cancer cells, but they can also affect the body in broader ways, sometimes leading to side effects like fatigue, nausea, hair loss, and changes in mood or appetite. Each person's experience is unique, so remember that it's okay to feel however you're feeling.

Reflective Prompts for Radiotherapy and Chemotherapy

What feelings do I have about starting or continuing treatment?

Whether you feel hopeful, fearful, anxious, or resigned, it's important to allow space for all your emotions. Write down what you're feeling as you face the next phase of your treatment.

How has my treatment impacted me physically?

Reflect on the changes you may be experiencing in your body. Are there specific side effects that are harder to cope with? Do you notice moments of strength or recovery that bring you hope?

What support do I need during this time?

Whether it's physical help at home, emotional support from family and friends, or professional guidance from healthcare providers, think about the kind of assistance you need to help you through treatment.

What is one thing I can do to care for myself during this treatment?

Sometimes it's easy to focus solely on the treatment itself, but self-care during this time is equally important. Whether it's resting, eating well, or finding moments of joy, write down one way you can show yourself love and care during this process.

Coping with Treatment Side Effects

Chemotherapy and radiotherapy often come with difficult side effects, both physically and emotionally. Here are some tips for coping:

Managing Fatigue:

Fatigue is a common side effect of both treatments. It's okay to rest more than usual and ask for help with everyday tasks.

Dealing with Nausea and Appetite Loss:

If nausea or appetite changes are part of your treatment experience, talk with your doctor about medication options. Eating smaller, more frequent meals can also help.

Caring for Your Mental Health:

Treatments like chemotherapy and radiotherapy can take a toll on your mental well-being. It's important to lean on your support system—whether it's family, friends, or cancer support groups—to talk through your feelings and gain strength from those around you. Sometimes, it takes a bit of homework to find the right support. For example, it took me a year to get invited to a local group for people with metastatic breast cancer! Don't be discouraged if it takes time. The right community is out there, and it can make all the difference.

Your Story, Your Treatment

Radiotherapy and chemotherapy can be long and tiring journeys, but each step is part of your larger story. Even on the hardest days, remind yourself that you are resilient and capable of facing what's ahead. Whether you've just begun treatment or are nearing the end, honour how far you've come and take pride in your strength.

ADDITIONAL PROMPTS FOR REFLECTION

What have I learned about myself during treatment?

Facing radiotherapy or chemotherapy can reveal new aspects of your resilience and inner strength. Reflect on what you've learned about your ability to endure and persevere.

What moments of lightness or joy have I experienced during this process?

Even during tough treatment days, small moments of joy—whether a favourite meal, a conversation with a friend, or a quiet moment of peace—can be powerful. Write down any moments of light you've experienced.

Affirmations for Radiotherapy and Chemotherapy

"I am strong enough to face this treatment, one day at a time."

"It's okay to rest and allow my body to heal."

"Even in hard moments, I trust that I am doing what's best for my health."

"I embrace the support of those around me, knowing I don't have to do this alone."

Chapter 3

Managing Medication: Finding Balance and Support

Medication can play a crucial role in managing illness, but it often comes with its own challenges, from side effects to emotional adjustments. Whether you're starting a new treatment, adjusting dosages, or dealing with long-term side effects, it's important to approach this aspect of your care with patience and self-compassion.

Tracking Your Medication

Keeping track of what medication you're taking, how it makes you feel, and any side effects you experience can help you stay informed and in control. Here are some questions to reflect on as you manage your treatment:

What medications am I currently taking?

Write down the name, dosage, and frequency of each medication. This can help you keep track of your regimen and ensure you're following your treatment plan.

What side effects am I experiencing?

Many medications come with side effects that affect your daily life. For me, my medication causes diarrhoea, nausea, and extreme fatigue. I've also had episodes of being sick out of the blue with no warning. After talking with an oncologist—although I don't always see the same one each time—they prescribed tablets to help manage these side effects. These tablets have been a huge relief, especially when I feel sickness may suddenly occur.

What support options do I have for managing side effects?

Dealing with side effects like diarrhoea can be difficult, especially when you're out in public.

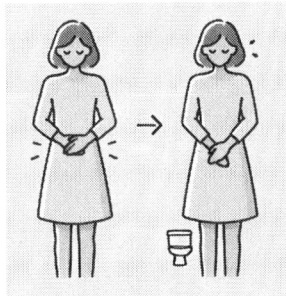

Thankfully, charities like Macmillan offer practical support. I discovered that they provide a card you can order online, which allows you to show staff in public places that, because of your cancer treatment, you may urgently need access to a toilet. This has been incredibly useful when I needed access to staff toilets or other restricted facilities.

You can order the official **Macmillan Toilet Card** online by visiting their website:

be.macmillan.org.uk

Simply search for "Macmillan Toilet Card" to find the page and place your order.

Note:

I have also created and included my own **Toilet Access Card** in this book that you can cut out and use. It may be helpful in situations where you need quick access to facilities. However, for a more formal card, I recommend ordering the Macmillan version as mentioned above.

PillTime: Making Medication Easier (UK Only)

While I don't use it myself, I know someone who does, and they've found it incredibly helpful. **PillTime**, partnered with the NHS in the UK, delivers pre-sorted, daily-dose pouches of medication directly to your door. Each pouch is clearly labeled with the date and time, making it so much easier to keep track of medications, especially if you're dealing with multiple prescriptions.

From what I've heard, it really takes the pressure off having to remember what to take and when. If managing your medication feels overwhelming, PillTime might be worth looking into.

You can visit their website for more information or ask your GP if it's available through the NHS in the UK.

Blue Badge Scheme (UK Only)

Even though I don't drive myself because I'm registered blind, having a **Blue Badge** has still made a big difference in my life. My partner uses it when driving me to appointments or outings, and it helps us park closer to where we need to go. For me, the Blue Badge has been especially useful with mobility challenges related to my sight and cancer treatment.

Some hospitals also offer dedicated parking bays for chemotherapy and radiotherapy patients, making it easier for those undergoing these treatments to park closer to the cancer centre. Since I'm not currently on those treatments, I use the disabled parking bays, but it's often a long walk to the cancer centre.

The Blue Badge allows parking in disabled bays, for longer periods, and closer to your destination, offering a little relief when dealing with medical appointments or daily tasks. If you think you might be eligible, you can apply through your local council's website. The process might take a bit of time, but it's definitely worth it.

Finding Support: You Are Not Alone

Navigating medication and its side effects can feel isolating, but you don't have to go through it alone. I found it helpful to connect with others on the same medication through social media. These groups offer a space to share experiences, advice, and encouragement from people who truly understand what you're going through.

Have you found others going through the same journey?

Whether through social media, local support groups, or online forums, connecting with people on similar treatments can provide valuable insight and comfort. Sharing tips on managing side effects or learning about others' experiences may help you feel more in control of your own journey.

What questions do I have for my doctor or oncologist?

It's okay to have questions or concerns about your medication. Speak with your healthcare provider about how you're feeling, especially if you're struggling with side effects. Even if you don't see the same oncologist each time, you can still receive valuable guidance, just like I did when I was prescribed medication to ease my nausea and tummy issues.

Coping with Side Effects

Managing side effects like fatigue, nausea, or diarrhoea can be challenging, but there are ways to cope that might make things easier:

Symptom Journal: Track when side effects occur, their severity, and what you were doing at the time. This might help you identify patterns and discuss potential solutions with your doctor.

Practical Adjustments: For me, having a walking stick has helped me manage fatigue, especially when I'm out and feel weak. Additionally, knowing I have tablets for nausea and tummy problems gives me peace of mind. Explore ways to make your daily life more manageable.

Your Story, Your Medication

Everyone's journey with medication is different. Some days, it might feel like the medication is helping; other days, it may feel overwhelming. It's okay to feel unsure or frustrated. The key is to listen to your body, be gentle with yourself, and reach out for support when you need it.

Reflective Prompts for Medication Management

Use these prompts to reflect on your experience with medication:

How do I feel about my medication?

Reflect on your emotional response to your treatment. Are you hopeful, anxious, or conflicted?

What side effects have I noticed, and how have they impacted my life?

Explore how your medication affects your daily life and well-being. Do certain side effects, like fatigue or nausea, impact your ability to move or enjoy your day?

What support systems can I lean on?

Whether it's family, friends, healthcare professionals, or online communities, think about who you can turn to for help.

Affirmations for Medication Challenges

Here are some affirmations for when managing medication feels particularly difficult:

"I am doing the best I can with the treatment I have."

"It's okay to feel frustrated or tired. I am strong enough to face this."

"I trust that I can find the support I need as I navigate this treatment."

Please Help!

PLEASE PROVIDE URGENT

TOILET ACCESS DUE TO MY

MEDICAL CONDITION

THANK YOU FOR YOUR UNDERSTANDING

Please Help!

PLEASE PROVIDE URGENT

TOILET ACCESS DUE TO MY

MEDICAL CONDITION

THANK YOU FOR YOUR UNDERSTANDING

Chapter 4

Facing Surgery: Navigating the Emotional Journey

Surgery is often a pivotal moment for those of us facing illness. Whether you are preparing for surgery or reflecting on a procedure that has already passed, the feelings it brings can be complex and layered. For some, surgery is a step toward healing; for others, it may carry deeper emotional weight.

My Personal Story: Surgery and Unexpected Turns

When I was first diagnosed with breast cancer, I was told it was stage 1. The doctors were optimistic, saying that after my breast removal, I'd be okay within a year. At the time, the idea of surgery didn't feel overwhelming—it seemed like a necessary step toward recovery. But after the follow-up scans, my world shifted. They found cancer in my lungs, and I learned I was facing stage four, not stage one. The certainty I once felt about being "okay" crumbled.

Later, I underwent surgery to have my ovaries removed. The decision was made to lower my oestrogen levels, but the emotional impact was much heavier than I expected. Having something healthy removed from my body felt strange—unfair, even. What upset me most was the finality of it: I would never be able to have children. While I try to focus on the positive—no more periods—the sense of loss still lingers.

Your Story: Preparing for or Reflecting on Surgery

If you are about to undergo surgery, you may feel a mix of hope and fear. And if you've already had surgery, you might be reflecting on the experience and how it has shaped your life. Surgery can be both a relief and a loss, a step toward healing and a reminder of what we've had to sacrifice.

Consider these questions as you prepare for or reflect on your own surgery:

How do I feel about this surgery?

Take a moment to sit with your emotions. Are you hopeful, anxious, or a mix of both?

What am I losing or gaining through this procedure?

Surgery can often feel like a trade—whether it's the removal of a tumour, an organ, or something else, think about what this procedure means for your life moving forward.

Who can I lean on for support?

It's important to acknowledge that you don't have to go through this alone. Whether it's family, friends, or healthcare professionals, who in your life can help you carry this emotional burden?

What fears or uncertainties do I have?

It's okay to feel afraid or uncertain. Name those fears, and consider how you might face them with courage and compassion.

Post-Surgery Reflections: Living with the Aftermath

If you've already had surgery, it's common to feel a range of emotions in the aftermath—relief, grief, confusion, or even anger. These feelings are valid. Healing is not just physical; it's emotional too.

How do I feel about the changes in my body?

Whether visible or invisible, surgeries often leave marks on us, both physically and emotionally. Take time to acknowledge those changes and how they make you feel.

What have I gained or lost?

Surgery might bring physical healing, but it may also bring a sense of loss, like the ability to have children or changes to your identity. Reflect on what you've gained through this experience, and also on what you may be grieving.

How can I honour my body's resilience?

No matter the outcome, your body has been through something significant. How can you take time to celebrate your strength, even if you're feeling uncertain or worn out?

Affirmations for Those Facing Surgery

In moments of fear or uncertainty, these affirmations may offer comfort:

"I am brave for taking the steps I need for my health, even when they are difficult."

"I honour my body for its strength and resilience."

"It's okay to feel sad, angry, or uncertain about this journey. I give myself permission to feel all of it."

Chapter 5

Your Personal Vision Statement

Creating a personal vision statement is a powerful way to clarify your aspirations and set the tone for your journey. It's your own guiding light, helping you stay focused on what truly matters to you.

Let's dive in!

1. Reflect on Your Dreams

Take a moment to imagine your ideal life. What do you want to achieve? How do you want to feel? Write down your thoughts:

2. Identify Key Themes

Look at your reflections and identify common themes. What stands out to you? Highlight key words or phrases that resonate:

3. Crafting Your Statement

Using the themes you've identified, start crafting your vision statement. Aim for a few sentences that encapsulate your dreams and values. Here's a fun prompt to help you:

"I envision a life where I am [insert feelings or experiences], achieving [insert goals], and surrounded by [insert people or environments]."

Example: "I envision a life where I am vibrant and full of energy, achieving my health goals, and surrounded by supportive friends and family who uplift me."

Complete your draft on the following page:

_____

Example 2:

"I envision a life where I find peace and joy in each day, surrounded by love and comfort, feeling grateful for the moments that matter."

If you need more space to write, I've left extra pages at the end of the chapter for you to use.

4. Make It Inspiring!

Read your statement aloud. Does it inspire you? If not, tweak it until it feels just right. Add positive adjectives and exciting verbs that energise you.

5. Visual Reminders

To keep your vision alive, consider creating a vision board! Gather images, quotes, and symbols that represent your goals and display them where you'll see them daily.

Ideas for your vision board:

6. Revisit and Revise

Your vision statement can evolve as you grow. Set a date to revisit it, and don't hesitate to make changes that reflect your new dreams or experiences.

Notes	Next Review Date:

A Note on Compassion

As you embark on this journey of setting goals and crafting your personal vision statement, it's important to approach yourself with kindness and compassion. Remember, this book is for you—whether you're facing illness or other life challenges.

There's no pressure to fill in every section or to set goals that feel out of reach. Life can be unpredictable, and it's perfectly okay to focus on what feels manageable and meaningful for you.

Allow yourself the grace to take small steps, or even to pause and reflect without the expectation of achievement. Your journey is unique, and every effort counts, no matter how big or small.

4. Your Personal Vision Statement

Craft a short, inspiring statement that captures your dreams

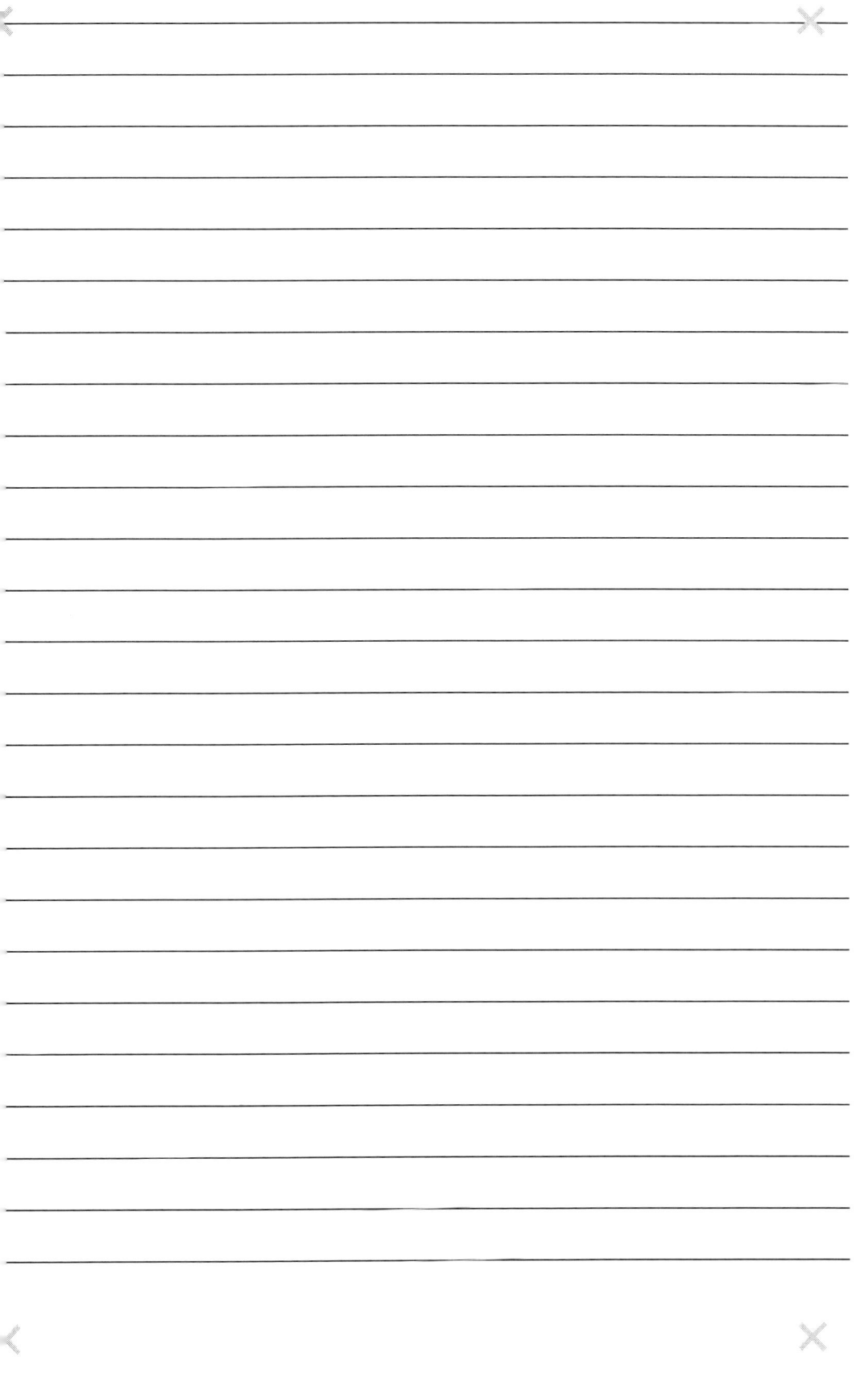

Chapter 6

Finding Inspiration in Small Moments

In the hustle and bustle of life, it's easy to overlook the small moments that can bring us joy and inspiration. When facing challenges, it becomes even more crucial to recognise and appreciate these little gems. This section encourages you to slow down, reflect, and find inspiration in the everyday.

1. Embrace Mindfulness

Mindfulness is the practice of being present in the moment. By tuning in to your surroundings, you can discover beauty and inspiration in the simplest things. Try taking a few deep breaths and observe what's around you right now.

What do you see, hear, and feel?

How can you appreciate these sensations?

2. Keep a Gratitude Journal ✿

Writing down things you're grateful for can help shift your focus to the positive aspects of your life. Each day, jot down at least three small moments that brought you joy or made you smile:

3. Celebrate the Little Wins 🎉

Every small achievement counts! Whether it's completing a task, enjoying a warm cup of tea, or sharing a laugh with a friend, take a moment to celebrate these victories. Acknowledge how they contribute to your overall well-being:

4. Seek Inspiration in Nature

Nature can be a powerful source of inspiration. Spend time outdoors, even if it's just in your garden or a nearby park. Observe the changing seasons, the sound of birds, or the way sunlight filters through the leaves.

What feelings does nature evoke in you?

How can you bring a bit of nature into your daily routine?

5. Connect with Others

Sometimes, inspiration comes from the people around us. Share your thoughts and experiences with friends or join a community of like-minded individuals. Hearing others' stories can spark new ideas and perspectives.

Who inspires you?

How can you deepen your connections with others?

6. Create Rituals

Establishing simple rituals can help you find inspiration in your daily life. This could be a morning coffee routine, an evening walk, or a few moments of quiet reflection. Rituals create a sense of structure and allow you to focus on the present.

What rituals can you incorporate into your day?

How do these rituals make you feel?

Embracing Inspiration

As you journey through life's ups and downs, remember that inspiration often hides in the small, everyday moments. By cultivating mindfulness and gratitude, you can transform ordinary experiences into sources of joy and motivation. Embrace the beauty around you, celebrate the little wins, and connect with others to enrich your journey. In these small moments, you may discover the strength and inspiration to keep moving forward.

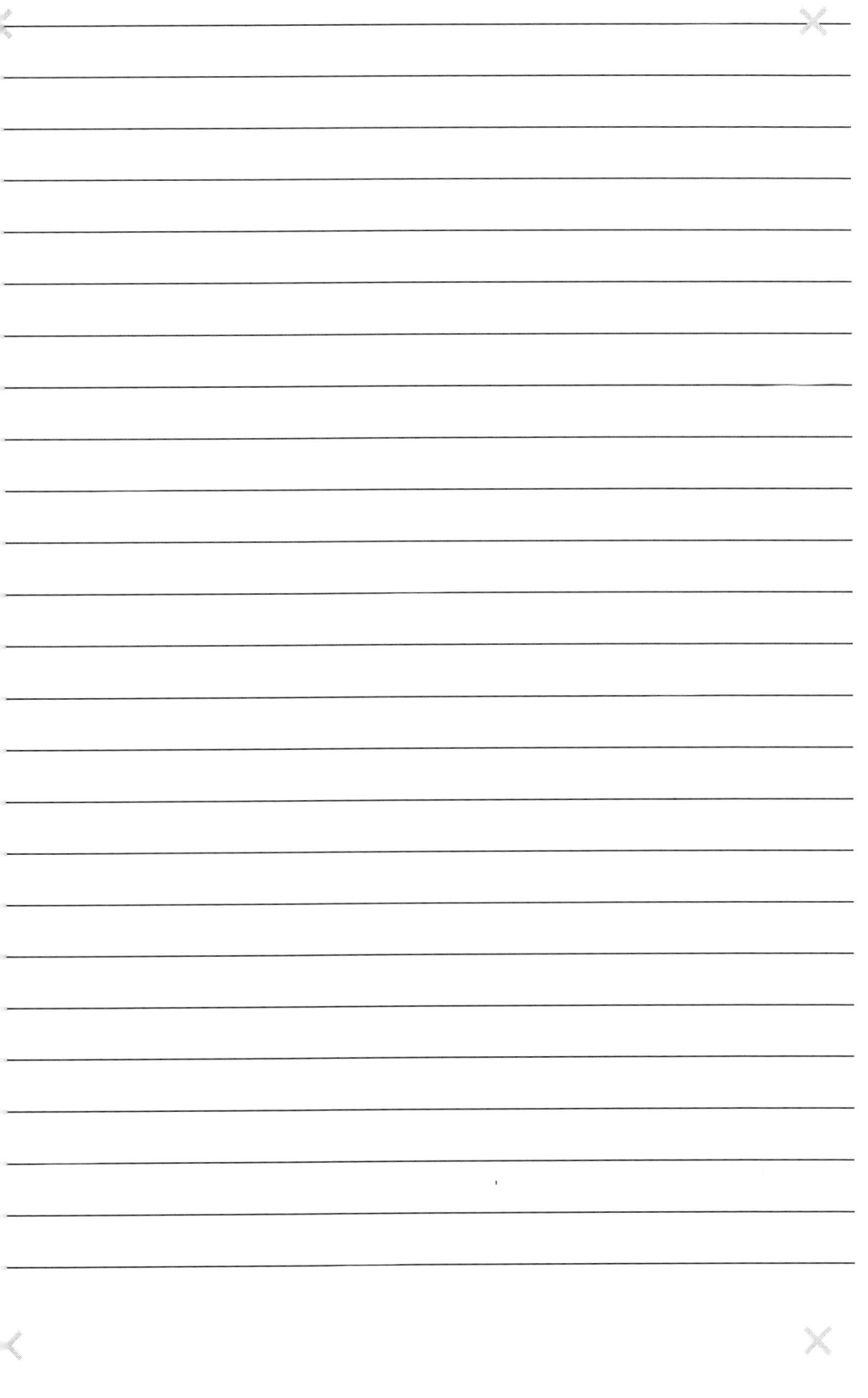

Chapter 7

Embracing Change

Change is an inevitable part of life, and while it can often feel daunting, it also brings opportunities for growth, learning, and new experiences.

This section invites you to shift your perspective on change, recognising it as a natural and essential aspect of your journey.

1. Acknowledge Your Feelings 😟 😃

It's normal to experience a mix of emotions when faced with change—fear, excitement, uncertainty, or even sadness. Take a moment to acknowledge how you feel.

Write down your thoughts:

Shift Your Perspective

Try to view change as an opportunity rather than a setback. Since my cancer diagnosis, I've realised how important it is to embrace life fully. I've been fortunate to find charities that offer experience gifts, such as holidays, which have allowed me to travel more and create lasting memories.

Ask yourself:

What can I learn from this situation?

How can this change lead to new possibilities in my life?

3. Embrace Flexibility

Being adaptable can help you navigate change more smoothly. For me, this has meant being more open to invitations and experiences. Consider what flexibility means for you and how you can incorporate it into your daily life:

4. Take Small Steps 🚶

When facing significant changes, breaking them down into smaller, manageable steps can make the process feel less overwhelming. Identify one small action you can take today to embrace the change:

5. Find Support

Reach out to your support network during times of change. Sharing your thoughts and feelings with friends, family, or support groups can provide comfort and new perspectives.

Who can I talk to for support?

What resources are available to help me navigate this change?

6. Reflect on Past Changes 🕰️

Think about previous changes in your life and how you adapted. What strategies helped you cope? Reflecting on your past successes can empower you to tackle new challenges:

_____

_____

_____

_____

_____

7. Practice Self-Compassion

Be gentle with yourself as you navigate change. Recognise that it's okay to feel unsure or anxious. Treat yourself with kindness, allowing space for your feelings:

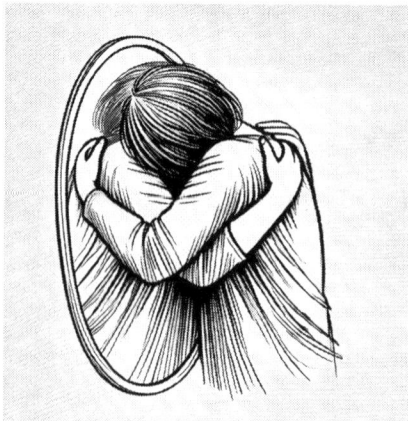

- How can I show myself compassion during this transition?
- What affirmations can I remind myself of?

Chapter 8

Creating Your Personal Goals

Setting personal goals can be a meaningful way to focus your energy and intentions, especially during challenging times. This section will gently guide you through the process of defining your goals in a way that aligns with your values and current circumstances.

1. Reflect on What Matters Most

Take a moment to think about what truly matters to you right now. Your priorities may shift, and that's okay. What are your passions, interests, or values?

Write down a few key areas you'd like to focus on during this time:

2. Set Clear and Specific Goals

When defining your goals, aim for clarity. Specific goals can help you maintain focus. Instead of saying, "I want to feel better," try: "I want to take a short walk every day if I feel up to it." Write your specific goals below:

Goal 1:

Goal 2:

_____

3. Make Goals Measurable

To help track your progress, consider how you will know when you've made progress toward your goals. This can be as simple as noting how often you achieve a small task:

✏️ Goal 1:

_____

✏️ Goal 2:

_____

4. Ensure Goals are Achievable

While it's great to have aspirations, it's important to ensure that your goals are realistic given your current situation. Reflect on any obstacles and how you might adapt your goals as needed:

🚀 Goal 1:

🚀 Goal 2:

5. Align Goals with Your Values

Check if your goals resonate with what you truly care about at this moment. Goals that reflect your values can bring a sense of purpose and fulfilment, no matter how small they may seem:

🔑 Goal 1:

🔑 Goal 2:

6. Set Time-Bound Objectives

Consider establishing gentle timelines for your goals, understanding that flexibility is key. Write down a timeframe that feels comfortable for you:

⏰ Goal 1:

⏰ Goal 2:

7. Create an Action Plan

Break your goals down into small, manageable steps. Identify specific tasks you can undertake at your own pace to move closer to your goals:

Steps for Goal 1:

Steps for Goal 2:

8. Review and Adjust Regularly

Life is dynamic, and so are your goals. Set aside time to review your progress regularly, and remember that it's perfectly okay to adjust your goals as your circumstances change:

Notes	Next Review Date:

Chapter 9

Shifting Sands: How Friendships Change During Illness

Denial and Distance

One of the hardest moments came when I was quietly left out of team selection for the county cricket team— a team I had helped start. Cricket had always been more than just a game; it was a shared passion that I had helped bring to life. It connected me to friends and gave me a sense of belonging. So, when I was no longer considered for selection, even though I felt well enough to play, the exclusion stung deeply.

There was no discussion, no acknowledgment—just a slow, painful realization that I was no longer part of something I had built. It wasn't just about missing the game; it felt like I was grieving the loss of a part of my life. And it wasn't just the cricket team. The grief also extended to my body, after having my ovaries removed to lower estrogen levels. It felt like a double blow—a reminder that my life had changed beyond recognition.

Lately, I've also noticed my hair falling out, but I've been fortunate to have thick hair, so no one has really noticed but me. Still, it's there—clumps coming out in the brush, strands gathering in the plughole. It's a subtle, constant reminder of how my body is changing. And I know that for some of you reading this, hair loss may be even more apparent. You may have lost your hair entirely. How has that made you feel? Do you embrace it, or have you chosen to wear wigs? There is no right or wrong way to handle it—only what feels best for you.

Both losses weighed heavily on me, reminding me that illness doesn't just change your body; it changes your relationships, your identity, and the things you once took for granted. I was grieving, not just my health, but the life I thought I'd always have.

But I knew I couldn't stay in that grief forever. With a history of depression, I understood how important it was to shift my focus to something that would keep me going. That's when I turned to writing this book. It wasn't just a distraction—it became my way of making sense of everything I was going through. Writing gave me purpose, something to work towards, and a way to help others facing similar challenges. In a way, it became my lifeline, giving me the strength to keep moving forward.

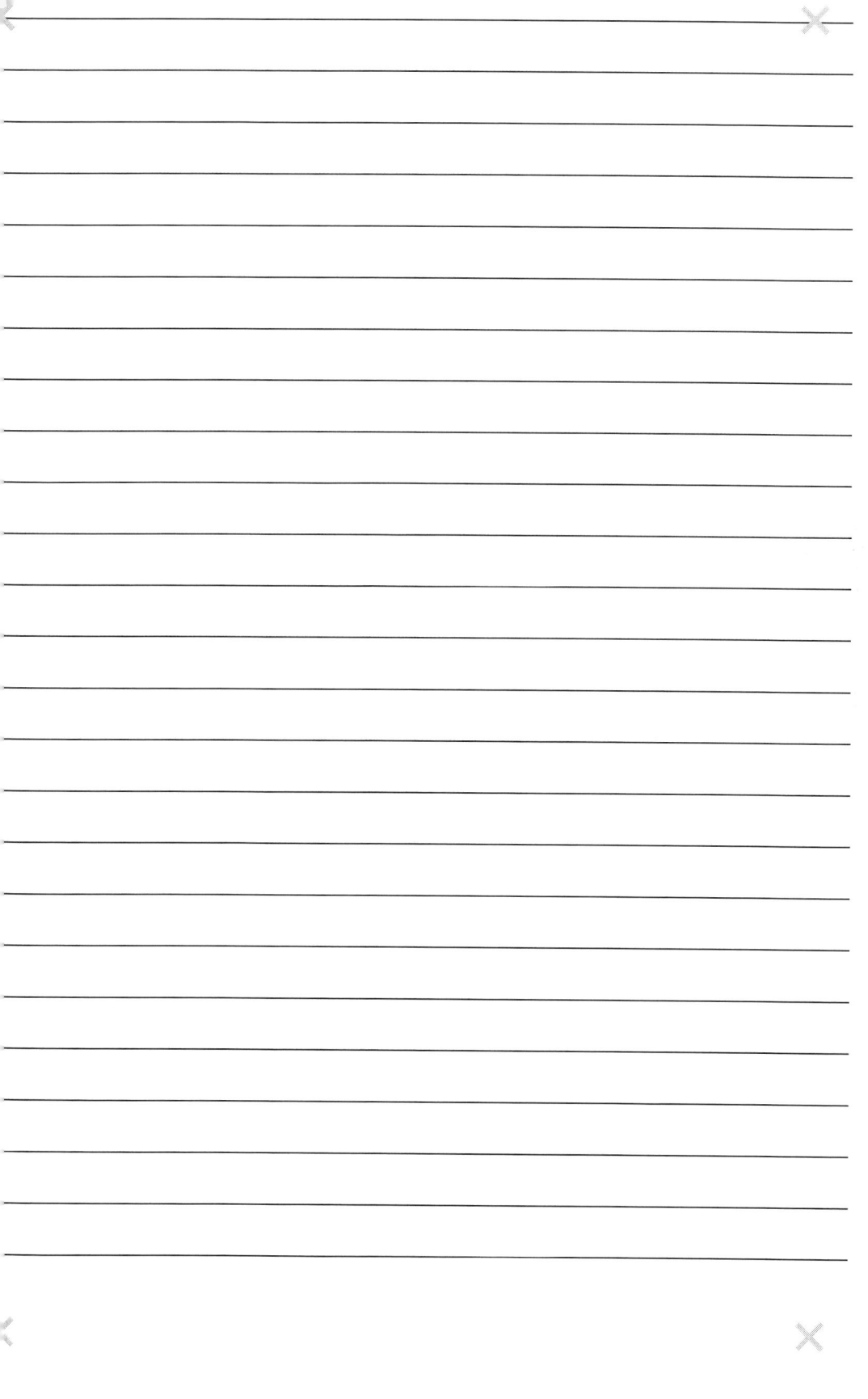

Chapter 10
Setting Realistic Milestones

Just as writing became my way of moving forward, I realised how important it is to break down larger, overwhelming goals into smaller, manageable steps. Life doesn't follow a straight path, especially when illness or unexpected challenges throw everything off course. It can feel like walking on shifting sands, where progress feels uncertain and unsteady.

Setting milestones became my way of navigating that uncertainty. By focusing on one small step at a time, I was able to regain a sense of direction and purpose. I didn't have to know the whole path; I just needed to take the next step. That's what I want to help you do in this chapter—find those small steps that will guide you toward your larger goals, no matter how daunting they may seem.

By breaking down your goals into achievable milestones, you can maintain motivation, track your progress, and remind yourself that each step forward matters. This section will guide you in establishing realistic milestones that support your journey, helping you find your way, even when life feels uncertain.

1. Understand the Importance of Milestones

Milestones serve as checkpoints along your journey, helping you stay focused and motivated. They provide a sense of accomplishment and help you measure your progress, making the overall goal feel more attainable.

2. Break Goals into Smaller Steps

Start by taking each goal you've set and breaking it down into smaller, actionable steps. Consider what you need to accomplish to reach each goal. For example:

◎ Goal: "I want to improve my physical activity."

Milestone 1: Engage in seated exercises for 5 minutes every other day.

Milestone 2: Increase to 10 minutes of stretching or gentle movement after one week.

Milestone 3: Try a new activity, like chair yoga or a gentle online workout, by the end of the month.

3. Make Milestones Measurable

Each milestone should have a clear, measurable outcome. This allows you to track your progress and celebrate achievements along the way:

Milestone 1:

Milestone 2:

4. Set Timeframes for Each Milestone

Assign a realistic timeframe for each milestone to help create accountability. Understand that your pace may vary, especially during challenging times, and adjust as needed:

⏰ Milestone 1:

_____

_____

_____

_____

_____

⏰ Milestone 2:

_____

_____

_____

_____

5. Celebrate Achievements

Take time to acknowledge and celebrate when you reach a milestone, no matter how small. Recognising your progress can help maintain motivation and reinforce positive behaviour:

🎉 How will I celebrate?

CELEBRIATE
SMALL WINS

CANCER

6. Reflect and Adjust

As you work toward your goals, be open to reflecting on your milestones. If something isn't working, it's okay to adjust your milestones to better fit your needs and circumstances:

What adjustments might I need to make?

What is one small milestone you've reached that made you proud?

How can you continue building on that success?

Chapter 11

Staying Motivated

Staying motivated, especially when dealing with illness or life's challenges, can be difficult. However, with the right mindset and support, it's possible to keep moving forward. Here are some tips to help you maintain your motivation, even on tough days.

1. Focus on Your "Why"

When the going gets tough, remind yourself why you set your goals in the first place. What drives you? What positive outcomes do you hope to achieve?

My reason for setting this goal:

How will achieving this goal improve my life?

2. Celebrate the Small Wins

Every small achievement counts. Taking time to celebrate these little victories can help you stay focused on the progress you're making, no matter how minor it may seem.

🎉 What recent milestone can I celebrate?

🏆 How will I reward myself for this achievement?

3. Surround Yourself with Support

Having a strong support network is essential. Surround yourself with people who encourage you and cheer you on during tough times.

👥 Who are my cheerleaders?

💬 How can I connect with them when I need encouragement?

4. Take Breaks When Needed

Remember, it's okay to rest. Allow yourself time to step back and recharge when things feel overwhelming.

🌿 What self-care activities help me recharge?

🌸 How will I incorporate rest into my routine?

5. Visualise Your Success

Take a few minutes each day to picture yourself reaching your goals. Visualisation can be a powerful tool to keep you motivated and focused.

How will I feel when I achieve my goal?

What will this success look like?

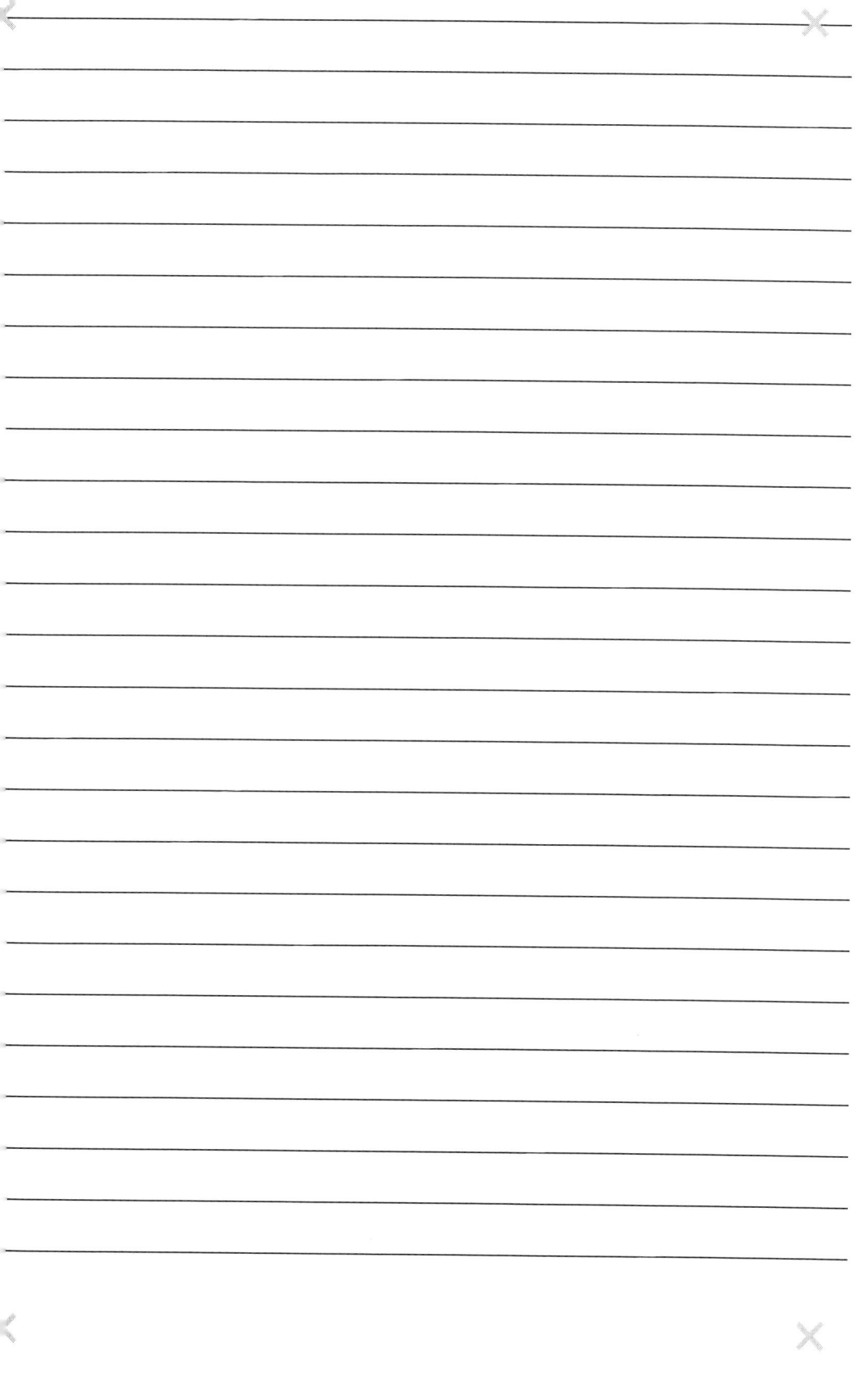

Chapter 12

Managing Setbacks

Setbacks are a natural part of any journey, and they don't mean failure. When facing obstacles, it's important to be kind to yourself and view these challenges as opportunities to grow and adjust your approach.

1. Acknowledge the Setback

It's important to recognise when something hasn't gone as planned. This allows you to address it head-on without self-blame.

⬡ What recent setback did I experience?

How did this setback make me feel?

2. Learn from the Experience

Every setback has something to teach us. Reflect on what went wrong and how you can adjust moving forward.

🔍 What can I learn from this situation?

📙 How can I use this lesson in the future?

3. Adjust Your Plan

Sometimes, setbacks mean we need to tweak our goals or timelines. Be flexible and adjust your plan if needed.

✏️ What adjustments can I make to my goal or milestone?

📝 What new timeframe feels realistic for this goal?

4. Stay Positive

Setbacks are temporary. Staying positive can help you push through and keep moving forward.

What positive affirmations can I remind myself of?

How will I refocus my energy in a positive direction?

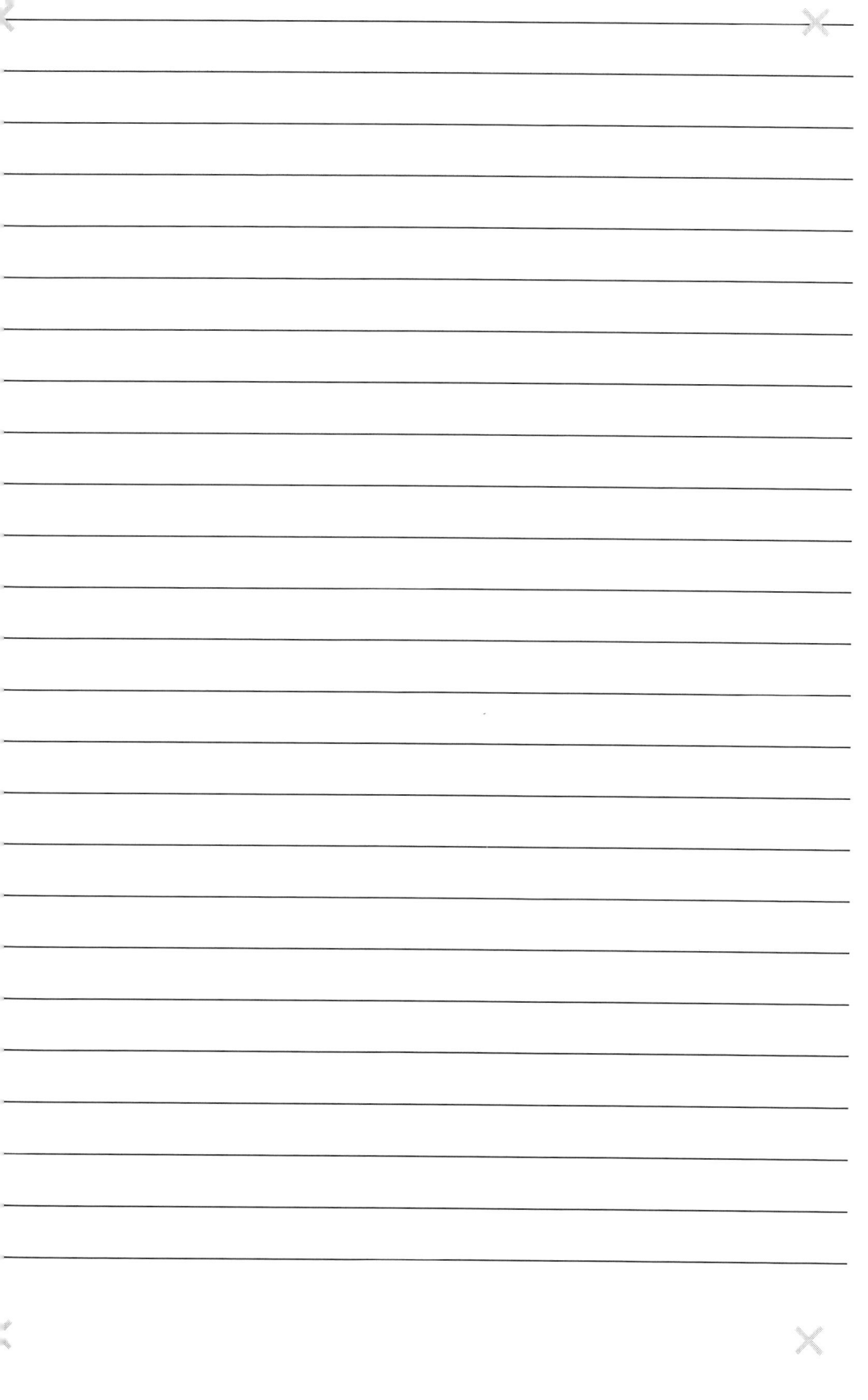

Chapter 13

Celebrating Success

Reaching your goals, big or small, is an achievement worth celebrating! Taking the time to acknowledge your successes not only boosts your confidence but also encourages you to keep striving toward new milestones.

1. Reflect on Your Achievements

Take a moment to reflect on how far you've come and all the progress you've made.

◎ What goal did I achieve recently?

How does it feel to have accomplished this?

2. Share Your Success

Sharing your accomplishments with others can deepen the sense of fulfilment. Don't hesitate to let your friends and loved ones know about your progress.

Who can I share my success with?

💬 How will I celebrate with my support network?

_____

_____

_____

_____

_____

3. Reward Yourself

Rewards don't have to be big or extravagant; they just need to bring you joy. Choose something meaningful to you to celebrate your hard work.

🎁 How will I reward myself for this achievement?

_____

_____

_____

_____

_____

4. Set New Goals

Success is a great time to think about your next adventure. Use the momentum from your achievements to set new goals for yourself.

✂ What new goal excites me now?

_____

🚀 How will I start working toward it?

_____

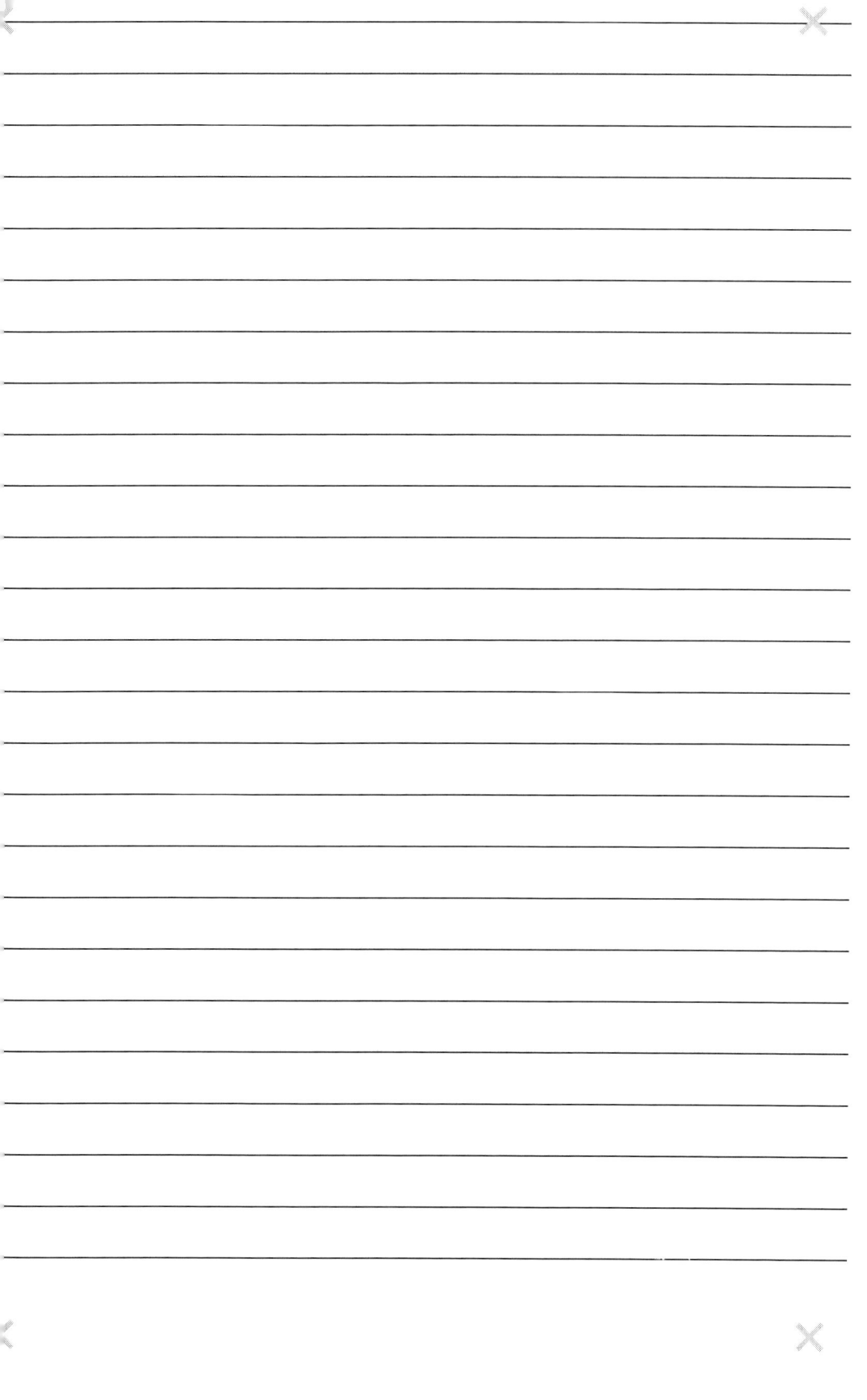

Chapter 14

Self-Reflection and Love

When facing life's challenges, it's easy to focus solely on getting through each day, forgetting the importance of self-love and reflection. This section is a space for you to pause, look inward, and embrace the person you are in this moment.

Self-Reflection Prompts

Taking time to reflect on your journey can provide clarity, healing, and peace. Here are a few prompts to help you explore how you've grown, what you've learned, and how you can continue to nurture yourself:

What have I learned about myself during this time? Consider the ways you've surprised yourself or shown strength in unexpected moments. Reflect on your personal growth.

What am I proud of today?

No matter how small or simple, acknowledging your victories—whether it's getting out of bed, enjoying a meal, or just making it through the day—is powerful.

What does love for myself look like right now?

Love can be quiet or bold. Think about how you can show yourself kindness and understanding in this season of life.

Self-Love Practices

Loving yourself doesn't mean having everything figured out. It's about accepting who you are at every stage and giving yourself the grace to continue.

Here are some ways to practice self-love:

Daily Affirmations: Begin your day by affirming your worth. Even on hard days, speak gentle truths to yourself:

"I am enough."
"I deserve care and compassion."
"I am doing the best I can."

Celebrate Yourself: Make a list of qualities you love about yourself. Think about your inner strength, your kindness, your ability to persevere.

Don't just focus on what you can do, but who you are.

Small Acts of Kindness: Show love by doing something kind for yourself. It could be a quiet cup of tea, a short walk in nature, listening to a favourite song, or simply allowing yourself to rest without guilt.

Affirmations of Love

In moments when you feel disconnected or unworthy, returning to these affirmations can remind you of the love and care you deserve:

"I am worthy of love, no matter the challenges I face."
"I choose to honour my journey and give myself the love I need."
"I deserve kindness, from others and from myself."

Reflective Journaling

Reflective journaling has been an important part of my life, especially during my time in counselling courses. It was a healthy practice that allowed me to process my emotions and explore not just how I felt, but why I felt that way. It also helped me understand how and why others made me feel a certain way. Journaling gave me the space to reflect deeply on those interactions, which was invaluable for my personal growth.

Use this space to reflect on moments of love—both from yourself and from others. Here are some questions to guide your journaling:

How have I shown love to myself during this time?

Reflect on any small or big ways you've taken care of yourself, whether through self-care, rest, or simply allowing yourself to feel emotions.

How do I want to grow in love for myself?

Think about the areas where you'd like to show more love or kindness to yourself. Maybe it's being gentler with your expectations or celebrating small wins.

What moments of love have I experienced from others that I can treasure?

Reflect on the love and support you've received from family, friends, or caregivers. Treasure these moments and allow them to uplift you.

Reflective Journaling Page

How have I shown love to myself during this time?

Reflect on any small or big ways you've taken care of yourself—through self-care, rest, or simply allowing yourself to feel emotions.

Your reflections:

How do I want to grow in love for myself?

Think about areas where you'd like to show more kindness to yourself—perhaps being gentler with expectations or celebrating small wins.

Your reflections:

. . .

What moments of love have I experienced from others that I can treasure?

Reflect on the love and support you've received from family, friends, or caregivers, and how these moments uplifted you.

Your reflections:

Feel free to use the extra pages at the end of the chapter if you need more space for your thoughts.

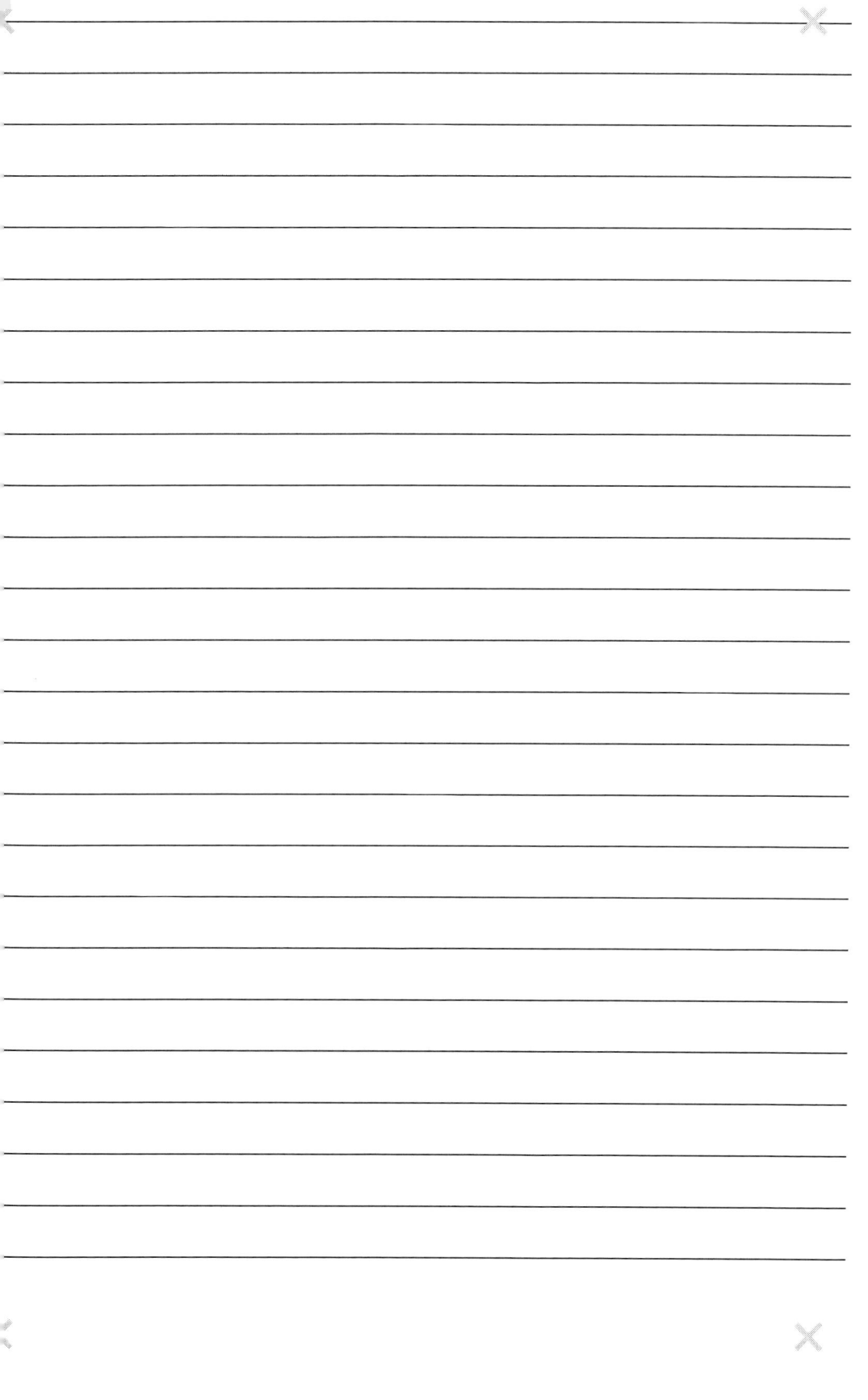

Chapter 15

Moments of Colour and Calm

I'll be honest, colouring has always been a bit of an adventure for me, considering my lack of sight. If you're anything like me, staying inside the lines is more of a suggestion than a rule—and that's perfectly okay! These pages aren't about perfection; they're about enjoying a bit of creative chaos and letting yourself unwind.

Whether you're filling these in during a peaceful moment or using them as a way to take a break from life's challenges, I hope they bring you a sense of calm (and maybe a laugh when the colours end up where they weren't supposed to!). So grab your favourite pencils, markers, or whatever you've got, and have fun. There's no right or wrong here—just enjoy the chance to add a little colour to your day, however it turns out.

I've only added a couple of colouring pages here, as this isn't really a colouring book, but I hope they inspire you to maybe go and grab a full one! Sometimes letting loose with a bit of colour is exactly what we need to take a break and reset.

Chapter 16
This Is Me

Sometimes, in the middle of all the serious stuff, it's important to remember the funny, quirky, and downright unique things that make us who we are. This section is designed to capture the essence of you—the things that make your loved ones smile and remember you with warmth and laughter. Fill it in however you like, and leave it for your family and friends to enjoy.

Get to Know Me Questions

What's the weirdest food combination I secretly love? (Maybe it's chips and chocolate or something even stranger—go on, confess!)

If I could be any animal for a day, which would I choose? And why? (Maybe you'd love to be a bird soaring through the sky or a cat lounging in the sun.)

What's my most ridiculous talent? (Can you wiggle your ears? Make the perfect pancake flip? Share something quirky!)

What's the funniest thing that's ever happened to me? (Tell a story that still makes you laugh when you think about it.)

If I could time travel, would I go to the past or the future? (Are you a history buff or more interested in futuristic gadgets?)

What's my favourite joke or pun? (Give your loved ones a reason to smile when they read this!)

What's the silliest thing I've ever done in public?
(Maybe you tripped over a curb, walked into a door, or got your coat stuck somewhere awkward—embrace the fun!)

If I could have dinner with any famous person (dead or alive), who would it be? (Is there a historical figure or celebrity you'd love to chat with over a meal?)

What's my go-to karaoke song? (Even if you'd never actually get up and sing, what's the song that'd get you up on the stage in an alternate universe?)

What's one thing about me that always surprises people? (Maybe you can juggle, or perhaps you have a hidden passion for collecting postcards—share something unexpected!)

Anything Extra?

Here's your chance to add anything else you'd like— something that didn't come up in the questions but you'd love for your family to know or remember about you. Feel free to write a little P.S. for your loved ones!

P.S.: By the way, I once sang at the Royal Albert Hall in London

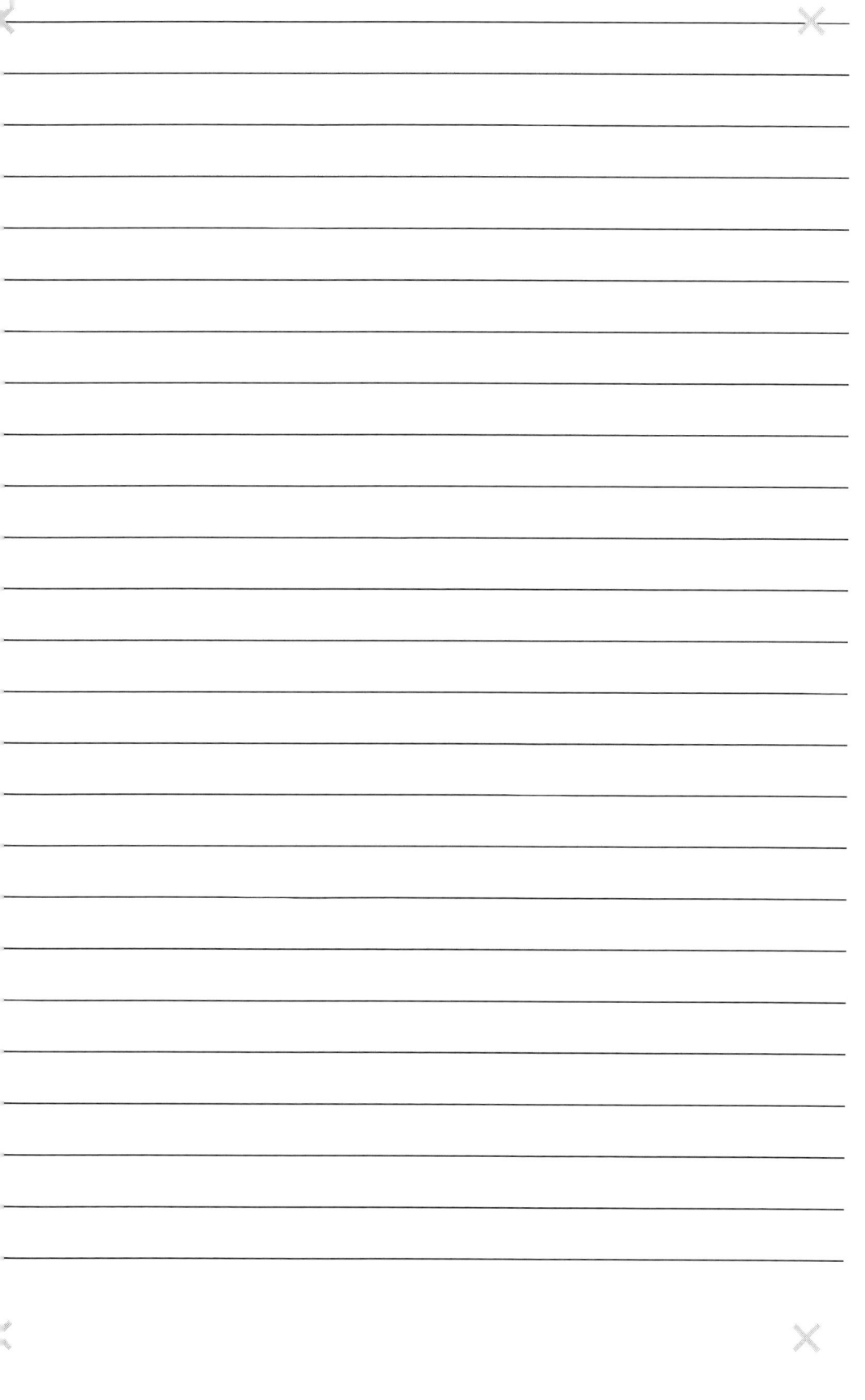

Chapter 17
A Note from Heidi

As I come to the end of this book, I want to take a moment to share something personal. If you had told me a few years ago that I'd be writing a book, I wouldn't have believed you. But life has a way of pushing us in unexpected directions. I wouldn't be writing this book if it weren't for my diagnosis of cancer. Being at home during this journey gave me the time and space to finally pursue my dream of writing. This book became a way for me to channel my energy into something positive—something that I hope has been valuable for you.

What's been most important to me throughout this process is ensuring that you, the reader, are getting good value for your time and money. I've poured my heart into these pages, and I truly hope you've found the content meaningful, inspiring, and helpful as you set your goals for the future.

Big hugs from me as we part ways for now. But before I go, I want to let you know that I'm already working on another book—one that focuses on something very personal to me: how to navigate Christmas with cancer. The holidays can be a tough time, but I want to share ideas on how to celebrate differently and still find joy in your own way, even during challenging times.

If you've enjoyed this book or would like to share feedback—or if you're interested in hearing more about my upcoming projects—I'd love to hear from you. Feel free to reach out at journeywithheidi@icloud.com.

Thank you so much for taking this journey with me, and here's to finding moments of joy, even in the most unexpected places.

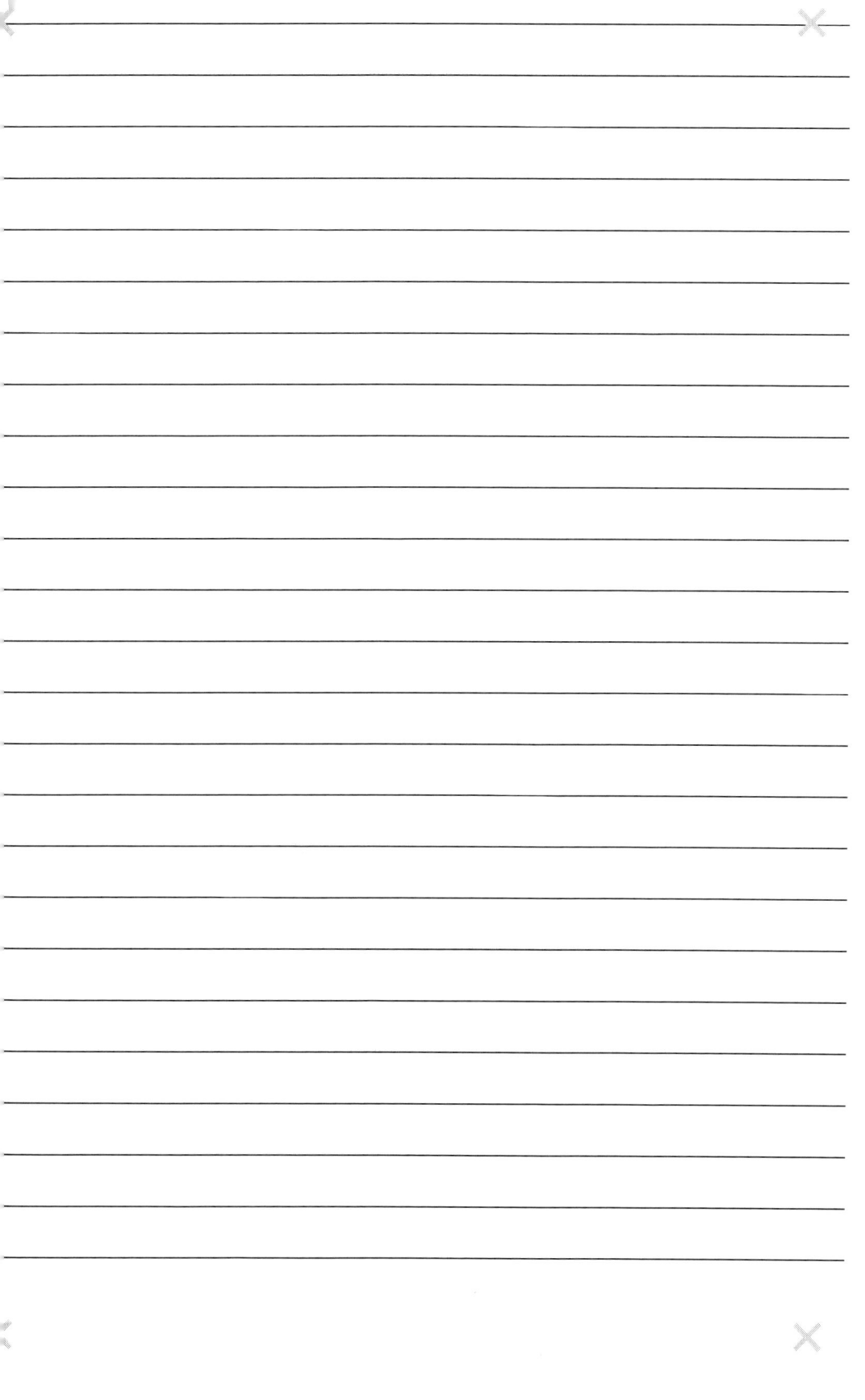

Acknowledgments

This book was a personal journey, and I'd like to thank myself for the perseverance and dedication it took to bring it to life. And thanks to my partner for supporting me on this journey. Special thanks to my two pets, Jasper (my cat) and Dave (my Axolotl), for giving me lots of distraction, breaks, and cuddles — especially Jasper, who doesn't like me being on the computer!

Support and Resources

Breast Cancer Care. (2024). *Support and Information for Those Affected by Breast Cancer*. URL: www.breastcancercare.org.uk

Breast Cancer Now. (2024). *Information and Resources for Breast Cancer*. URL: www.breastcancernow.org

Cancer Research UK. (2024). *Understanding Cancer and Treatments*. URL: www.cancerresearchuk.org

Macmillan Cancer Support. (2024). *Support for Cancer Patients and Families*. URL: www.macmillan.org.uk

Maggie's Centres. (2024). *Free Cancer Support and Information Across the UK*. URL: www.maggies.org

Marie Curie. (2024). *Care and Support for People Living with Terminal Illness*. URL: www.mariecurie.org.uk

NHS. (2024). *Cancer Support and Treatments*. URL: www.nhs.uk

The Royal Marsden. (2024). *Information and Care Resources for Cancer Patients*. URL: www.royalmarsden.nhs.uk

Something to Look Forward To. (2024). *Gifts and Experiences for People with Cancer*. URL: www.somethingtolookforwardto.org.uk